Brave Little Shepherd

1 Samuel 17:34-37 retold by
TERRY WHALIN

illustrated by
ANDY STILES

STANDARD
PUBLISHING
Cincinnati, Ohio

"You are my God, and I will thank you."

Psalm 118:28

The Standard Publishing Company, Cincinnati, Ohio
A division of Standex International Corporation
© 1996 by The Standard Publishing Company
Printed in the United States of America
Library of Congress Catalog Card Number 95-37054
Cataloging-in-Publication data available
All rights reserved. Designed by Coleen Davis
ISBN 0-7847-0452-X

In the little town of Bethlehem
in the country of Israel
lived a young shepherd boy.

David watched over a flock
of sheep for his father.

In the daytime, David found good grass for the sheep to eat . . .

and cool, clean water for them to drink.

At night, David counted his flock to make sure every sheep had come home.

Then he built a fire to keep
wild animals away.

Whenever the sheep were sleepy and full,
they lay down to rest near David.
They felt safe beside their gentle shepherd.

Sometimes a small lamb wandered away from the flock, chasing a butterfly.

Then David took the crook of his walking stick and guided the lamb back to its mother. "There, little one, don't wander off!" said David.

"Stay nearby where I can see you. Then you won't get into trouble." David swooped up the lamb and gave it a squeeze. The lamb's soft wool felt nice against his face.

While the sheep were grazing and resting, they could hear David strumming his harp and singing. David's songs were full of praise to God.

He thanked God for the sun that warmed his back in the day. He thanked God for the moon, so big and round in the starry sky.

He thanked God for taking care of him just as a shepherd cares for his sheep. David's songs were like a wonderful gift that David gave to God. He sang them over and over to the Lord.

David was gentle, but he was also brave.
He was always ready to protect his sheep
from danger.

Sometimes when the sheep were resting,
David practiced throwing stones with his sling.

One afternoon, David was singing his songs while the sheep lay around him, resting. Suddenly, at the edge of the flock, the sheep began bleating, "BAA! BAAA!"

David put down his harp.
"What's wrong with the sheep?" he wondered.
David put a stone in his sling as he looked
around the field. Then he saw —

A BEAR!

The bear had a lamb in its powerful arms and was dragging the lamb away for supper.

"BAAA!" cried the lamb.

Though David was young, he wasn't afraid.

"God, help!" he quickly prayed as he ran toward the bear.

Then he threw the stone in his sling with all his strength.

ZING!

The stone hit the bear right
between the eyes.

The bear fell to the ground
and dropped the little lamb.

David and the little lamb were safe!

David hugged the little lamb.
"Thank you, God," he said. "I knew you would help me. You are always with me."

Brave but gentle, David put his trust in God.